Teddy Bears
Fun with Words

Illustrated by Ann and Mike Ricketts

Brimax · Newmarket · England

Cycling

The teddy bears are cycling,
The wheels turn round and round;
They like to race each other
As they ride along the ground.

Running

All the teddies have a race
They're running very fast;
Rosie is the winner
And Polly comes in last.

Swimming

Swimming in the afternoon
Is what Rosie likes the best;
She races Ben and Polly,
Then has to stop and rest.

Jumping

Altogether in the rain
The teddies want to play;
Jumping in the puddles,
Splashing all the way.

Gardening

The teddies work together
There's gardening to do;
Sam and Ben are weeding
And Rosie's helping, too.

Shopping

Shopping in the afternoon
Is always lots of fun;
The teddies buy the food they need
Then walk home in the sun.

Swinging

The teddy bears are swinging
Together in a row;
They have to hold on very tight
As higher up they go.

Reading

Reading in the midday sun
Under the big oak tree;
"Look at the pictures, Sam," says Ben,
"We can learn our ABC."

Baking

Polly and Sam are baking
A special birthday treat;
Chocolate cake and cookies
Which they all love to eat.

Painting

The teddies are painting pictures,
They're having lots of fun;
Blue is for the sky above
And yellow is for the sun.

Skating

The teddy bears are skating
Together in a row;
They like to hold each other's paws
As down the ice they go.

Hiding

One teddy plays a game for fun
Hiding behind a tree;
He counts to ten and looks around
To find the other three.

Skipping

Skipping in the garden
The ropes go round and round;
The teddies count, "One! Two! Three!"
As they jump off the ground.

Climbing

Climbing high up in a tree
The teddies stop to rest;
They like to watch the baby birds
Sitting in their nest.

Sliding

Playing in the snow is fun
The teddies all agree;
When sliding down a snowy hill
As quickly as can be.

Dancing

The teddies all like dancing
To the songs they know;
Rosie plays the violin
As round and round they go.

Washing

The teddy bears are washing;
The day is nearly through;
Together they all wash and splash
And clean their teeth, too.

Sleeping

The teddy bears are all in bed,
They are sleeping tight;
And through the bedroom window
The stars are shining bright.